The Legend of St Cuthbert

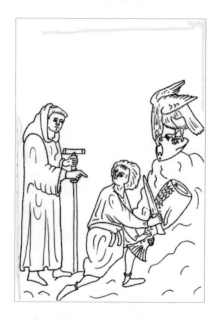

by Robert Hegge

In a Modern English Version

by Simon Webb

Durham, 2009

First published by Simon Webb, 2009
badgerbeard55@hotmail.com

ISBN: 978-0-9544759-6-3

Cover design by Miranda Brown.
The pictures show (front cover)
The Journey, depicting the last stage
of the saint's journey to the city.
The back cover shows *St Cuthbert.* Both
© 2008 Dr. Fenwick Lawson ARCA,
RIBA Northern (Hon), DLitt (hon).
Photographs supplied by Ananna Image.

1 INTRODUCTION

Now, Simon, said this John, by Saint Cuthberd
Aye is thou merry, and that is fair answer'd.

Chaucer, The Reeve's Tale

Robert Hegge was born in the city of Durham sometime around 1597. Like Leonardo da Vinci and the French artist Marcel Duchamp, he was the son of a notary. From the age of fifteen he was able to attend Corpus Christi College, Oxford, thanks to an annuity of £20 left to him by his grandmother. The grandmother, Anne Swyft, lived in Durham's South Bailey, and is known to have owned a 'figure of Sent Cudbert, with jewels and ivory'. Perhaps the memory of this glittering artefact inspired Robert to write his re-assessment of the city's saint.

At Oxford, Hegge distinguished himself by his scholarship and became a fellow of Corpus Christi in 1624. Apart from *The Legend of St Cuthbert*, his works include Latin verses and a treatise on sundials. He died of apoplexy in 1629, at the age of 32.

Hegge's *Legend* was first published in London in 1663. A second edition appeared in 1777. The 1816 Sunderland edition, edited by John Brough Taylor, is the basis for this book. I have also used the 1824 Durham edition, which was intended as a faithful representation of the 1777 version. There are significant differences between these two editions: I have tried to combine the best of both.

The full title of Hegge's book is *The Legend of St Cuthbert, with the Antiquities of the Church of Durham*. Hegge's choice of the word 'legend' suggests that he did not mean to provide a simple biography of the saint: he wanted to give an account of his reputation and its long-lasting effect.

Hegge probably chose to write about Cuthbert because he knew that without Cuthbert, Durham might never have become a city at all. The history of Durham and its cathedral is intimately linked to the life and legend of this seventh-century monk, priest, bishop and, sometimes, hermit or anchorite.

Hegge admires many things about Cuthbert, but he can't bring himself to believe in any of the miracles attributed to him either before or after his death. He suspects that cynical churchmen invented these miracle-stories as a way to gain more riches and influence. The author also disapproves of the saint's addiction to long periods of isolation. He thinks it is unhealthy and unnatural for a person to be away from other people for such a long time.

The acid of Hegge's scorn does not, however, tarnish the reputations of the good and learned men and women he praises in his *Legend*. He also appreciates the literature, scholarship, art and architecture the church has handed down to us, and laments the condition of what Shakespeare calls the 'bare ruin'd choirs'; the remains of the mighty monasteries that once dominated the English landscape.

Hegge clearly had a taste for the stiff, rattling parchment of old manuscripts, and he seems to have read everything on his subject that was available to him. His version of Cuthbert's story differs from that found in some of his sources, but then his sources also disagree among themselves. He augmented his book with details of tombs, stained-glass windows and other pieces of concrete evidence he had personally seen.

Hegge cannot resist peppering his text with bits of Latin, and other learned ornaments. He also wanders into digressions, and introduces personal details. Like many seventeenth-century prose writers, Hegge seems to love long sentences, punctuated with many colons and semi-colons. The grammar contained in these sentences is sometimes extremely convoluted. He uses some forgotten English words and phrases such as 'hally-wark' and 'weamb', and many words which have changed their meanings or associations since he wrote his *Legend* in 1626.

The aim of this modern English version is to convey Hegge's ideas intact, but in a form that will be easier for modern readers to digest. I have broken up his long sentences, simplified grammar and introduced shorter paragraphs. I have added sub-headings and substituted modern equivalents for obsolete words, or words that have changed their meanings. Sometimes I have added extra words and phrases in the interests of clarity. The story of St Gregory's encounter with the Deiri in Rome is very compressed in the original, and has been expanded here so that Gregory's complex Latin pun can be fully understood.

Some of the Latin phrases have been translated directly into English and silently dropped into the flow of the text. Longer quotations have been set out separately, and the sources noted (Hegge often assumes the reader will identify a Latin quotation without his help). Thanks are due to William Duggan, Kevin Hunt and C.C. Slater for help with the Latin.

Hegge tends to Latinise names so that, for instance, 'Turgot' becomes 'Turgotus'. I have changed these spellings back to the most common modern spelling, which is probably closer to what the people in question would have been called among English-speakers during their lives. Where Hegge gives only a surname, I have sometimes added the first name in the interests of clarity. Hegge always calls Cuthbert 'St Cuthbert' – I have changed this to 'Cuthbert' in some places.

For place-names, I have given the modern equivalents where possible, although some places mentioned cannot be linked to modern locations with any certainty. James Raine's 1828 book on St Cuthbert, Fowler's 1903 edition of the *Rites of Durham,* and South's 2002 edition of the *Historia de Sancto Cuthberto* contain many useful suggestions in this and other areas. Hegge calls Durham Cathedral either an abbey or a church – I have preferred to use 'Durham Cathedral' where possible.

There is clear evidence in the text that Hegge intended to revise it, not least to include extra details about the tombs in the precincts of Durham Cathedral. Where Hegge's text contains simple errors, I have corrected them. The most obvious example here is where Hegge states that Cuthbert performed *all* his miracles on the island of Inner Farne, then later states that *all* his miracles were performed after his death.

Illustrations marked 'JR' are from James Raine's 1828 book on St Cuthbert, and are based on miniatures in a twelfth century manuscript of Bede's *Life of Cuthbert* (British Library Yates Thompson MS 26). They are reproduced with kind permission from Durham County Council. The picture marked 'GA' is from the 1824 edition of George Allen's 1777 version, also reproduced with kind permission from Durham County Council. Photos and other pictures are by the author. Thanks to Joanna Lawson for help and advice on the images of Fenwick Lawson's sculptures used on the cover of this book.

FROM THE AUTHOR TO THE READER

Things dead and gone are subject to the judgement of the present and the future, and historians are permitted to steal from past authors, as long as they acknowledge their sources.

On my journey through this history, I first met up with the Venerable Bede, who told me he was eleven years old when St. Cuthbert died, and had written his biography using the best information he could get.

A little further on I met with Turgot, a Prior of Durham, who was an eyewitness to the miraculous preservation of St. Cuthbert's corpse. He had also inquired into the history of Lindisfarne and Chester-le-Street: Turgot was a great help to me on my journey. Later I overtook Laurence, a monk of Durham, who continued the story of Cuthbert where Turgot had left off.

Travelling on, I came upon Simeon, a native of my county of Durham: but Roger Hovenden told me the same tale as Simeon had. After this I had the company of William of Malmesbury, William of Newburgh, Albertus Parisiensis, Westmonasterynsis, and Ranulf Higden, who all travelled the same way as I did, and also told me stories about St. Cuthbert.

John Capgrave, a monk of Bury, told me about more wonders than all the rest; and a man called Nicholas, of Finchale, whiled away a few miles with his version of the story of Saint Godric.

When I had become almost completely lost, Nicholas Harpsfield's directions stood me in good stead, and many others also helped me to my journey's end.

ROBERT HEGGE,
DURHAM.

1st July, 1626.

HEGGE'S INTRODUCTION TO
THE LEGEND OF ST CUTHBERT

If you set history and prophecy back to back, they look like Janus, the two-faced god, who could see both the future and the past.

In history time lives after it is dead, and in prophecy time lives before it is born. Since only a god can see into the future, a man must be content to see into the past, and to observe it, as it were, through his grandfather's eyes.

This is the only immortality we can enjoy on earth; to make history the epitaph after the funeral of things, and to rescue memory from the grave that entombs its ashes.

I owe this duty to the place where I had my birth: to renew the decayed epitaphs upon the tombstone of its history.

I: BEFORE CUTHBERT

Geographers treat countries the same way that astronomers treat constellations: they imagine them into shapes. In this way, Italy becomes a man's leg, Spain becomes an ox's hide, and Britain becomes a hatchet.

Using the same method, the Bishopric of Durham becomes the Greek letter Δ, and the City of Durham becomes a crab: the city itself is the belly, and its suburbs the claws.

The county lies in the bosom of the North Sea, and is embraced by the arms of two crystal rivers, the Tees and the Derwent. The second of these rivers falls into the Tyne, and only arrives at the sea after it has lost its own name:

> Through lowly vales he cuts his winding way,
> And rolls his ruddy waters to the sea.
> *Lucan, The civil war, Book I, 398-9, Trans. Rowe*

In Roman times the inhabitants of this county were the Brigantes. The same people were known as the Deiri in Anglo-Saxon times[1]. When St Gregory was the archdeacon of Rome, he came upon some of these Deiri, who were being sold as slaves. The name of their tribe put him in mind of the anger of God (*De ira Dei* in Latin), and the fact that they came from the country of the Angles made him think of angels. When he heard that their king was called Aelle, Gregory spoke about alleluias as well, saying, 'The Angles, who look like angels, should learn to sing alleluia, and escape the anger of God'.

Following this encounter, Gregory persuaded Pope Benedict to send Augustine, the apostle of the English, to Britain to re-convert[2] the British.

The first of the Saxon kings of this region to be baptised as a Christian was Oswald. He brought his people the first fruits of holiness, and was a conqueror of both men and religion. William of Malmesbury says that Oswald was the first of the English race to become famous for miracles. King Oswald claimed that his victory over Cadwallon was accomplished because of the Cross of Christ, used as a standard by his army at the battle of Denisburne. This is the first cross we read of in English history.

---

1 The kingdoms of Deira and Bernicia were united to form Northumbria in the late 7th century AD.
2 Britain needed to be re-converted as it had been partly Christian in Roman times.

Oswald sent for a learned Scottish monk called Aidan to help him bring about the conversion of his people to Christianity. He made him Bishop of Lindisfarne, but because Aidan only spoke the language of the Scots, Oswald stood up and translated for him when he taught the people.

This great monarch, the pious founder of the mother church of the North, lost his life in a battle against the Pagan prince Penda. Oswald lost the battle, as well as his life. Penda cut off Oswald's head: after that, he could no longer wear an earthly crown, but he could wear the more glorious crown of martyrdom.   The rest of Oswald's body was torn into pieces, and his relics, 'too great to lie in any single place'[3], ended up in various places. So many churches claimed that they alone possessed the tomb of Oswald, it became like the competition between Greek cities for the title of cradle and birthplace of Homer. Part of his corpse was entombed in Bardney Abbey in Lincolnshire, and afterwards moved to Gloucester, where lately (not without some reverence for history) I myself viewed his shrine. It stands between two pillars at the upper end of the abbey, on the north side of the chancel.

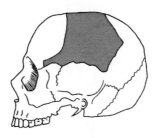

Skull thought to be St Oswald's,
found in Cuthbert's tomb, 1899.
Grey area shows head-wound which
was probably Oswald's death-wound

Oswald's head was brought to Lindisfarne, and then moved with St. Cuthbert's body to Durham Cathedral. His arm was preserved in a silver casket at Bamburgh, not far from Lindisfarne (Bamburgh was the capital of the region at that time).

Oswald's arm was miraculously preserved because Aidan had blessed it. According to Bede, Oswald was sitting at dinner one Easter day when a servant came in. The servant told the king that some poor people were

---

3   Epigrams of Martial, Book 5, no. 74 (about Pompey and his sons, who died in different parts of the world).

begging at his gate. Oswald ordered him to give the beggars all of his own food, together with the silver plate it had been served up on, which was to be divided between them. Aidan was so affected by this act of charity that he took the king by the hand, saying, 'May this arm never perish'.

After the death of Oswald, Aidan became so sad that he died of a broken heart. It was as if he thought it was a sin to carry on living after such a good king had died. Thus, the Pagans managed to kill both a king and a bishop with one stroke.

II: THE COMING OF CUTHBERT

Aidan's soul was carried up to heaven in the middle of the night, by a choir of angels. This was actually seen and heard by a young shepherd in the fields. He was so moved by what he saw that he resolved to become a monk at the monastery of Old Melrose; a place founded by Aidan on the banks of the river Tweed. The shepherd later became known as St Cuthbert.

The Devil didn't want Cuthbert to get to Melrose, and he tried to stop him; but Cuthbert gave him a good cudgelling and sent him on his way. If you are able to look through the lens of superstition, you can see the print of the Devil's cloven hoof in that very place to this day.

On his journey to Melrose, something else happened to Cuthbert, that showed his qualities of humility, devotion and gratitude. Overtaken by night and hunger, he was forced to enter an empty cottage where he found only a horse to welcome him. The horse turned up some hay and uncovered part of a loaf, which had probably been left there by a shepherd. Cuthbert said grace, and shared the bread with the animal.

Cuthbert slept in the empty cottage with the horse that night, and arrived at Melrose the next day. As soon as he approached, Boisil, the Prior of the abbey, seemed to see his future saintliness in his face, and ran to embrace him.

Boisil presented Cuthbert to Eata the Abbot, who made Boisil his tutor. Boisil taught Cuthbert to read from St John's Gospel. In honour of St Cuthbert, the copy they used was preserved at Durham in Prior Turgot's time, and was called the Book of St Cuthbert. Although it has existed for many centuries, no moth has ever dared to feed on it.

After he had lived the life of a perfect monk for fifteen years at Melrose, Cuthbert was promoted by Bishop Eata to the position of Prior of Lindisfarne.

Thanks to the royal charter of King Oswald, Lindisfarne became the mother church of the Bernicians during the time of Aidan. The Bishops of Durham are still regarded as the successors of Aidan of Lindisfarne.

According to a monk of Durham, Lindisfarne is only eight miles in circumference. It is an island only twice a day, at high tide: when the tide goes out, it shakes hands with with the mainland. On this Holy Island (so christened because of Cuthbert's sanctity) Finan, Aidan's successor, built a cathedral church of wood, thatched with reeds. This puts one in mind of the time when:

> Jupiter complete could barely stand in his low shrine,
> And the lightning bolt in his right hand was made of clay.
> They decorated the Capitol with leaves, not gems,
> And the senators grazed their sheep themselves.
> *Ovid, Fasti, bk 1, from l. 200, trans. A.S. Kline*

Soon Eadbert, Cuthbert's successor, replaced the holy thatch with lead. This showed both his devotion to God and his willingness to spend money;

though it is not the mason, but the worshipper, that makes a church.

There were fourteen bishops of Lindisfarne, among whom St. Cuthbert was regarded as the brightest star.

Ruins of Lindisfarne, c. 1820 (GA)

III: CUTHBERT BECOMES A PRIOR, THEN A HERMIT

Cuthbert was Prior of Lindisfarne for twelve years, and lived in such a state of holiness that the Devil was much grieved by his virtues. Once, when Cuthbert was preaching at a certain village, the Devil set fire to a house, in an attempt to draw the people away from his sermon. The country folk were amazed to find they could not put the fire out with water, but Cuthbert realized it was only fantastical fire, sent by the Devil.

In 676, after twelve years as Prior, Cuthbert resigned and became a hermit. He chose an island called Inner Farne for the place of his hermitage.

Inner Farne was as empty of trees, water, crops and people as it was full of devils, but it became the setting for many of Cuthbert's miracles. As soon as he arrived, the spirits who had made the island theirs flew away, giving up their title to the property. The rocks poured out fresh water, and the earth produced corn, although nobody had tilled the land. It was as if the Golden Age had returned.

Here Cuthbert gave up nine years of his life to contemplation. He was so wholly devoted to heaven that he forgot he was on the earth at all, and for a whole year he didn't even take off his shoes. He had no people to listen to him, so he preached to the birds that ate his corn, telling them not to hunger after what was not theirs by right. Indeed, his teaching to the birds was so effective that they never touched his harvest again.

He also cured two crows of the habit of stealing thatch from the roof of his hut, to make their nests. He made the crows feel so guilty about this that they lay down at his feet, begging for forgiveness. They also brought him a piece of pork as a way of saying sorry. These are only a few of the wonders Cuthbert performed, if we are to believe the legend.

Such stories are enough to demonstrate what advantage the monks took of the blind devotion of that age. They spent a lot of time and effort inventing and repeating tales of the miracles supposedly performed by saints. The stories were easily believed, because superstitious people will believe anything.

The monks called it a 'pious fraud' to make up these Christian miracles. They did it to impress the Pagans, but these days such stories just make people suspicious about religion. The monks should have known that truth has never needed the protection of lies – it will always win in the end, without any help from hypocrisy.

My digression is finished now, and I will return to St. Cuthbert on his island.

Here Cuthbert had so many fights with the Devil that you might be able to see the prints of the Devil's cloven hoof there even today, but only if you are able to look with superstitious eyes.

If any visitors came to Inner Farne to see Cuthbert, he quickly ran into his hermitage, and would only speak to them out of the window. It was only after much persuasion, and because of the great love he felt for Aebba, the virtuous Abbess of Coldingham, that he sailed to Coquet Island to see her. While he was there, he foretold King Ecgfrith's death to her. He also prophesied that Ecgfrith would make Cuthbert himself a bishop before he died. He even predicted the reign and the victories of King Alfred.

During his stay on Coquet Island, Cuthbert still went down to the shore to pray, as he always did. Someone who secretly watched him doing this saw two sea-monsters[4] come out of the sea, to kneel at his feet and worship him. These creatures would only go back into the sea when Cuthbert had given them his blessing.

---

4   In Hegge's sources, these are otters.

Cuthbert later returned to his hermitage. There, confined in his cell, his fame grew greater and greater as people saw less and less of him.

IV: CUTHBERT IS MADE A BISHOP

*The King visits Cuthbert on
Inner Farne (JR)*

At a synod held at Twiford upon Aln[5], in the presence of both King Ecgfrith and Archbishop Theodore of Canterbury, Cuthbert was made a bishop.

That he would become a bishop had been foretold about him when he was a boy, by a smaller child who was then only three years old. This child gravely warned him that it did not suit a bishop to play among children.

St. Cuthbert was so devoted to the solitary life that neither letters, nor ambassadors from the synod, could persuade him to take upon himself the responsibilities of a bishop. At last the king himself, attended by lords and nobles, sailed to his island. There were enough people with the king to invade a city, but all they were trying to conquer was Cuthbert's resolution.

Thus honour pursued a man who fled from it, and promotion came to a

---

5   Possibly Church Hill, Alnmouth or Whittingham in Northumberland.

man who had hid himself from it. How times have changed.

At that time, there was no Bishop at Hexham, so Eata gave up the Bishopric of Lindisfarne and went to Hexham instead. This left Lindisfarne free for Cuthbert. King Ecgfrith enlarged Cuthbert's diocese by adding most of the city of York, the abbeys of Melrose and Ripon, and also the village of Crayke and the city of Carlisle, with the lands around them. Cuthbert later built a nunnery at Carlisle.

St. Cuthbert's mind was, however, still on his hermitage, and he soon returned there. In 687 he died in his cell, and thereafter began to perform even more miracles.

If I had been asked to make a speech at the funeral of St Cuthbert, I would not have mentioned his having been a hermit, among his good points. To my mind, hermits become less than men, and meditate until they convince themselves that they are gods, or wild men, which shows more pride than religion. They say that a hermit is either a god or a beast, but I say a hermit is more likely to become a beast.

Hermits remind me of the condition of Nebuchadnezzar after God had cursed him. Nebuchadnezzar was driven away from humanity, and ate grass like an ox. His body was wet with the dew of heaven, and his ears became like eagle's feathers, his nails like the claws of birds. When a hermit excommunicates himself from being a citizen of the world, he sins against the common good, and makes himself unlike a man, because men are naturally sociable.

Others may think Cuthbert was showing devotion to God by being a hermit, but I think he was showing signs of melancholy madness.

V: CUTHBERT'S DYING WISH

St. Cuthbert's last wish was to be buried on the east side of his oratory on Inner Farne, in a coffin that the venerable Abbot Cudda had given him. He told the monks they would find the coffin buried to the north of his cell. He instructed them to wrap his corpse in a shirt that Verca, the Abbess of Tynemouth, had once sent him as a gift. Out of reverence for this holy woman, he had never worn the shirt during his life.

His last instruction to his monks was that if the area should be invaded by Pagans, they should take his bones with them when they fled. Thus St. Cuthbert made himself into a saint during his life, and gave the monks advance notice of what a precious relic his body would become when he was dead.

All these requests were duly carried out, except that the monks wept and begged to be allowed to take his body back to Lindisfarne. He was solemnly buried there, in a stone tomb in St. Peter's Church, on the right side of the high altar, in 687.

In those days, the widespread belief in miracles funded the construction of many churches, and religious houses multiplied to such an extent that the whole of England seemed to be just one great monastery. The Pope even called England 'The Land of Priests'.

Now Time, who is constantly eating the world, has so fed upon these ancient buildings, that she has completely devoured some, and picked others to the bone. What Time left standing has now been eaten up and defaced by deliberate destructiveness. One man who was responsible for much of this destruction was King Henry VIII.

Henry brought about the death of many churches, and defied the thundering anathemas threatened by the monks against the violation of abbey lands:

> If all of the many outraged gods should avenge their
> Godheads, you alone would not be enough for the punishment
> *Ovid, Heroides II, trans. James M. Hunter*

I am forced to mourn those abbeys, whose names are now lost and buried in their own ashes. Their very ruins suffer the death of a sepulchre and die twice, because there is no sign of their ever having existed.

Among the monuments of devotion to God that are still remembered (and once belonged to St. Cuthbert) are Coldingham, seated between Lindisfarne and Berwick. Both of these places were given to St. Cuthbert's monks by Edgar, King of Scotland, at the time of the Conquest. The monastery at Coldingham contained both monks and nuns: such was the chastity of those times. At one time Aebba was the abbess: she had received her veil from Finan, the second bishop of Holy Island.

At Alnwick there was a priory of Carmelites, or white friars, founded by John, Lord Vasey in 1240. He was the man who first introduced this order of monks to Britain.

The episcopal seat of Hexham, in the land of the Bernicians, was given to Cuthbert by King Alfred. William of Malmesbury praises the beauty of Hexham's architecture, saying that it is better than any other building on this side of the Alps. (Malmesbury mistakenly says that Hexham is only fifty miles from York.)

This sumptuous church was built by St. Wilfrid in 675, and endowed with lands by Queen Æthelthryth, wife of King Ecgfrith. In this church sat nine Bishops, among them the learned John of Beverley. John, who is not to be named without respect by an Oxford man, was made a bishop on the orders of King Ecgfrith. He was Bishop of Hexham until he went to York.

In his younger years, he was raised as a nobleman in the care of Hilda, founding abbess of Whitby in Yorkshire. Later, he was a student of that great man of learning, Theodore, Archbishop of Canterbury. Theodore, who was born at Tarsus in Cilicia, was the first to bring learning, coupled with religion, into England. It was Theodore who first brought Homer to Britain – an author we had not read before. He also brought the works of other good authors, and instructed many famous scholars in Greek and Mathematics. Among these were St. Bede, Herebald, Wilfrid, and John of Beverley.

When Theodore's school at Cricklade was moved to Oxford, John of Beverly became the first Master of Arts at the University. This is shown by an ancient window in Salisbury Library, which features a picture of John.

Anyone who tries to show that Oxford University pre-dates this time, will only be groping in the dark. Oxford's eight-hundred year history is enough to prove Cambridge University to be the younger sister. Leland argues that Sigeberht, king of the East Angles, founded that University, because Bede and Malmesbury say that he erected various schools in his kingdom. But neither author mentions either Granta or Cambridge, nor does any writer mention a university at Cambridge for another four hundred years after Malmesbury.

If the reader is a Cambridge man, he must pardon me for this digression.

VII: THE TOMB IS OPENED

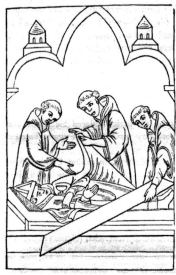

First opening of Cuthbert's tomb (JR)

To return to St. Cuthbert, who had now lain in his tomb for eleven years. The monks thought that by this time his body would be nothing but bones, so they decided to take the bones out and put them among their other relics, to be kissed and adored. They opened Cuthbert's coffin, and staggered back in wonder. They had expected bones, but found flesh. They expected a skeleton, and saw a complete body, the flesh so succulent, that a little heat would have made the body seem to live without a soul. The face was so unlike that of a dead man, that in this case, instead of sleep being the image of death, death was the image of sleep.

Cuthbert's funeral clothes were so fresh, it seemed that putrefaction had not dared to take him by the coat. It was as if, once God had received Cuthbert's soul, he had denied nature the opportunity to take his body.

Now Bede, who was eleven years old when Cuthbert died, reports the miraculous preservation of Cuthbert's body. In reporting this, he did not invent a lie, but he did repeat one. In writing his life of Cuthbert, Bede relied on information from the monks of Lindisfarne, who attributed to

Cuthbert all the miracles of the saints in scripture.

They were such empty-headed monks that they could not invent new miracles, but used any that came to hand. So, because Adam had commanded all the animals, Cuthbert had to have savage beasts paying him homage. Abraham could not entertain three angels under an Oak, but St. Cuthbert had to have angels for his guests, at the monastery of Ripon. The children of Israel ate manna and angels' food, so Cuthbert had to have three loaves given to him by an angel, which were supposed to have been baked in Paradise. A raven brought Elijah food, so an eagle had to bring St. Cuthbert fish.

If I am right, then the story of Jonah was used to concoct the tale of what happened when Cuthbert and his mother sailed from Ireland to Scotland.

It is said that a book of psalms fell into the sea from their boat. This was swallowed by a seal, which delivered the book up to them when they landed. If you substitute a man for the psalter, and a whale for the seal, then you have the story of Jonah.

With these, and many other such stories, the monks entertained the superstitious people of those times.

The celebrated miracle of the preservation of St. Cuthbert's body made the church so famous that King Ceolwulf, believing in St Cuthbert's holiness, forsook his royalty to become a monk on Lindisfarne. He brought with him so many royal treasures and donations of lands, that he seemed rather to resign his kingdom to the church, than to his successor. It was as if he became a monk just to make Cuthbert a king.

Ceolwulf gave Cuthbert all the land between the Tees and the Wear, and many towns and estates, such as Warkworth Castle, Cliffe, Billingham (where Bishop Ecgred built a church), Warkworth, Hutingham[6], Edlingham and Ellingham. I'm not sure if these towns have now died out, or if their names have changed.

Ceolwulf was very welcome to the monastery, because after he arrived the monks, who had previously only been allowed to drink milk or water, were allowed to drink wine or ale; although people who drank from St. Cuthbert's cup, after he had drunk from it, had sometimes found the water turned into wine, without a miracle.

After some years spent living as a monk, instead of living like a king, this devout monarch was entombed at Norham, in the church built by

---

6   Possibly Whittingham (Hwitingham in the anonymous *Historia de Sancto Cuthberto*.)

Bishop Egfride in 819. The castle in this town was built by Ranulf, Bishop of Durham, in 1099. Bede dedicated his *Ecclesiastical History* to Ceolwulf.

As well as persuading Ceolwulf to become a monk, the miraculous preservation of Cuthbert's body persuaded Bishop Eadfrid to place the saint in a new tomb, in a more prominent and impressive position, above the pavement in the sanctuary. It seems it was not thought fitting for him to be buried among the dead, when his body seemed to live without a soul, and to turn death into a sleep.

By this time, even the ground St. Cuthbert had trodden on was considered holy, and a church had been built at every place he had visited. Because Cuthbert had lived there, Bishop Eadfrid built on the site of his hermitage on Inner Farne. A monk called Ethelwald of Ripon lived there as a hermit for twelve years, as if some spirit of holiness still survived in the place from Cuthbert's time.

The monks of Lindisfarne flourished for many years, until the Danes disturbed their peace and prosperity. They began to make incursions into Britain, continuing their piracies and invasions until they made a complete conquest of King Harold. Harold was soon defeated by the Normans as well, which meant that England was conquered twice in seventy years.

In those days many old monasteries, which had been erected by pious people, were cremated, and entombed themselves in their own ashes. At this time the famous Hartlepool Abbey perished, where the religious Hieu had built a nunnery[7]. I think I may say of this town, as Hildebert[8] said of Rome, 'Her ruins show how great she was in her glory'. Now travellers can see in her a monument to both piety and conflict.

The two monasteries of St. Peter and St. Paul, at Wearmouth and Jarrow respectively, were also destroyed in those days. They were built by two Abbots, Celfride and Benedict, at the spot where the famous River Wear flows into the ocean. These communities were so firmly united by mutual brotherhood, that they seemed like one monastery in two places. They will remain famous as long as educated people still remember the Venerable Bede, because it was in these monasteries that he had his first education, under Benedict.

---

7   Hieu was abbess of a joint house of both monks and nuns at Hartlepool.
8   Hilderbert of Lavardin (1055-1133) wrote two celebrated poems about the city of Rome.

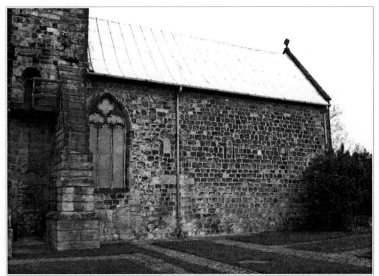

The Saxon end of St Paul's Church, Jarrow - heart of the Jarrow monastery. Note tiny windows to the right, intended to house small pieces of glass.

Benedict was a reverend abbot, who is rightly remembered as someone who obtained choice books for his monastery from overseas. He was also the first person to bring the use of glass windows for churches into England. Before his time, church windows were only glazed with cloth.

In his riper years (as I said before) Benedict had been instructed in both sacred and secular learning by Theodore, Archbishop of Canterbury. Under his instruction he acquired such maturity of judgement, that no writer since has brought greater honour to his nation.

Although Benedict confined himself to his cell, his fame travelled to Rome. Pope Sergius wrote a letter to Abbot Celfride, begging Benedict to come to Rome in person. But as far as I can tell from my reading, Benedict never accepted the Pope's invitation, and died at Jarrow. During his last illness, he translated St John's Gospel into English. This was a heinous crime for Roman Catholics in those days, when the people were supposed to find their way to heaven wearing a blindfold: only priests were allowed to see the way clearly.

In honour of its association with Benedict, his monastery was re-built by a monk called Aldwin, after it had been laid waste by the Pagans. Once they had been revived, these monasteries carried on until they were moved to Durham.

Remains of the second monastery at Jarrow

VIII: THE MONKS FLEE

The fury of the Danes increased, and their attacks spread south to Tynemouth, where St. Cuthbert's friend Verca had once been abbess. Their proximity to Tynemouth forced the monks of Lindisfarne to look about them. The loss of some neighbouring monasteries made them realise that the Danes would not (like the Devil) be frightened away with holy water. They also saw that it was not safe to trust entirely to the protection of a saint.

The monks decided in favour of flight, a course of action that Cuthbert had recommended to them, if they were ever overrun by Pagans. They put all their relics into St Cuthbert's tomb, and ran away in 893, leaving the Danes nothing but an empty church.

It was the bad luck of Eardulf to be Bishop during these troublesome times. He followed behind St Cuthbert's body with his clergy, together with whole families of the lay people who had been attached to the monastery.

Cuthbert was carried by monks, who were the designated escorts of the body. They were the only people allowed to touch the coffin: anyone else who did so would suffer Uzzah's punishment[9].

You might think these miseries would have made people doubt Cuthbert's sainthood. Although they were pursued by foreign foes, and a home-bred enemy called Famine, Cuthbert could not help his followers. They were driven to the Irish Sea, and might have complained, as the ancient Britons did to Aetius the Roman consul, 'The barbarians drive us to the sea; the sea drives us back to the barbarians: between them we are to choose two sorts of death; we are either slain or drowned'[10].

Since the Irish Sea would not part for them, the Bishop decided to sail to Ireland with a small party of monks, hoping to find a resting-place for St. Cuthbert's coffin in the land where he had been born[11].

They had not sailed far from the shore when the winds and the waves were up in arms against their pinnace. The gods of the sea and wind should have worshipped their vessel, since it contained a bishop, his clergy, and so many relics that it was more like a cathedral than a ship. But the sea didn't have enough religion to hear their prayers, and threatened them with a terrible shipwreck. As a result, the monks didn't have enough confidence in their saint to encourage the sailors, as Caesar did his, by saying, 'Fear not: you carry Cuthbert!'[12]

Cuthbert now needed another saint to pray to for help, as he was in danger of being drowned after his death. If this had happened, where would the future church of Durham have been, and the devotion of kings to Cuthbert's sepulchre? Where would the tutelary deity against the Scots have been, and the church lands called 'St. Cuthbert's patrimony'? If St. Cuthbert had been entombed in the sea (and forced to erect his bishop's seat among the fish) the future tenants of his lands would have had to pay tribute-money. They would also have been obliged to serve in time of war, instead of just feeding fat, easy-living monks for so many years.

This sacrilegious storm infected the ship with such a palsy, that it shook

---

9 Uzzah was slain for touching the Ark of the Covenant (2 Sam. 6:6).
10 From Chapter XIII of Bede's *Ecclesiastical history*.
11 The tradition that Cuthbert was born in Ireland is represented in a twelfth century book called the *Libellus de ortu sancti Cuthberti*.
12 Refers to an incident in Plutarch's *Life* of Julius Caesar.

a book of the four gospels into the sea. This was a volume that Bishop Eadfrith of Lindisfarne had written with his own hands in honour of St Cuthbert; and Belfrid the anchorite had decorated it with detailed illuminations and gilding.

The monks were great experts in this art of illustrating books, and knew how to enchant the eyes of the common people. Such works are ingenious and commendable, but they do suggest that the monks had a lot of time on their hands.

It may be that the sea grew stormy because it wanted St Cuthbert for itself, or it may be that Cuthbert himself raised the tempest because he didn't want to go to Ireland. In any case, the sea and the winds eventually conspired to bring them back to the place from which they had set off.

You may imagine that there was great joy at their arrival, but also great sorrow because of the drowned book; until Hundredus, one of the seven escorts of the body, was told by St. Cuthbert in his sleep to search on the shore at Whithorn. There he found the book in its former beautiful state, without a single blemished letter.

This book was kept in the church of Durham in Prior Turgot's time, in memory of the miracle when the water seemed to run out of itself, to do homage to St. Cuthbert. It seemed the water would rather lose its nature, than wet Cuthbert's book.

If this is true, then I am sure St. Cuthbert's books had much better luck in the sea than they have now in his library at Durham. The place was once a little Vatican of choice manuscripts, but is now more of a tomb for books than a place to conserve them.

Since the art of printing was invented, and people could get some superficial learning both cheaply and easily, old manuscripts have been bequeathed to the moths. Now pigeons and jackdaws are the only students in church libraries, and people use penknives to cut the pictures out of the books. This reminds me of the cruelty shown to St John Cassian, or John Scotus Erigina, who were both martyred by their own students.

Hundredus the monk had another night-time visit from St. Cuthbert, who said he should go to a tree, on which he would find a bridle. As soon as he saw the bridle, a dun horse would appear, and offer to pull the wagon on which they should lay Cuthbert's coffin. The monks did not steal the horse, you understand: it was a horse provided by St Cuthbert.

They followed this horse wherever it drew the cart. At length, by the guidance of the horse (or St. Cuthbert) they came to Crayke, where for four months they were kindly entertained by the abbot, and had time to tell stories of their travels.

Here, again in a dream, St. Cuthbert played the Pope. He sent Eadred, Abbot of Carlisle, and one of his followers, on an embassy to the camp of the Danes. Cuthbert instructed them to crown Guthred king there (Guthred had been sold to a widow as a slave).

What authority St. Cuthbert had to nominate a king, or what reason the army had to believe a dream, must be ranked among St. Cuthbert's miracles. In those days, even Popes couldn't dispose of kingdoms like that.

IX: CHESTER-LE-STREET

By becoming a king in this way, Guthred became nothing more than St. Cuthbert's subject, and was forced to be under a great obligation to the monks who had taken advantage of him. Under the protection of the new king, the monks regained their episcopal see of Chester-le-Street, where Eardulf became the first bishop.

Later, Eadred brought another dream-message from St Cuthbert to the king, telling him to give all the lands between the Wear and the Tyne to his church forever. He was forced to grant this modest request, to avoid the monks accusing him of ingratitude.

Thus the poor king received a crown, only to set it on St. Cuthbert's head. He was, in effect, robbed of his kingdom.

The monks also demanded that St. Cuthbert's church be given the status of a sanctuary: this meant that any criminal who reached his tomb would be granted sanctuary for thirty-seven days. In this way, magistrates and judges were prevented from curbing crimes against heaven and the state in those days. Sanctuaries just allowed people to offend in greater safety, and to appeal to a saint against the king and his laws.

Thus, the king was again cheated of his sovereignty by the monks, who now became experts at enslaving the devotion of kings for their own bad ends.

In 872 King Alfred the Great also swore to be loyal to St. Cuthbert and his clergy. They told him that it was through them he had scored a victory over the Pagans. Alfred also made a royal charter confirming the privileges King Guthred had granted to the monks. He also freed the inhabitants of St Cuthbert's lands from tribute to the king, and service in war. The charter also contained a fearful anathema against any of Alfred's successors who should dare to infringe the privileges of Cuthbert's people. This was another case of a king betraying his own majesty, and depriving himself of the service that is naturally due from a subject to a king.

Alfred also showed his respect for St Cuthbert by consecrating a chapel to the saint at University College, Oxford, of which Alfred is said to have been the founder. In an ancient window in that college I have seen King Alfred and St. Cuthbert painted together, the king saying to the saint, 'Here I have established a college in your honour', and the saint replying, 'I curse those who would ruin what you have established'.

By such curses, the monks held on to their lands much more securely than they would have if they had held them under the broad seal of the King.

I suspect that either St. Cuthbert was an angry saint, or the monks used his name to curse a lot. I say this because of two lines of verse carved into a wooden beam over the hall door of Trinity College, Oxford (sometimes called Durham College). This was built for a fraternity of monks by Thomas Hatfield, Bishop of Durham, in 1343 (he also built Durham House in London). The lines read, 'Those who are not afraid to plunder Cuthbert's lands will be certain to die an evil death'.

But to return to King Alfred's devotion to St. Cuthbert, with whom he was prepared to share his sovereignty.

Alfred even did Cuthbert the honour of including his name on his coinage. I know this because I have seen pictures of some silver coins dug up in Little Crosby in Lancashire in 1611. This money was sent to my friend the antiquary Mr Thomas Allen of Gloucester Hall, Oxford. The coins are stamped on one side with Alfred, and on the other with Cuthbert.

(JR)

26

Aerdulf, the last Bishop of Lindisfarne and the first of Chester-le-Street, shared both in St. Cuthbert's prosperity and his adversity. Later, he saw the flourishing state of the new church that arose, like a phoenix, out of the ashes of the former. At last he yielded to nature, full of days and honour, and was entombed at Chester-le-Street in 894.

In the same year the victorious Alfred also died. On his death-bed he left his love of St. Cuthbert as a precious legacy to his son Edward, instructing him to be as much the heir of his devotion to that saint, as he was to his kingdoms.

King Edward also zealously nominated his son Aethelstan to act as executor of his love for Cuthbert's church.

With the accession of this high and mighty King Aethelstan, the Heptarchy[13] came to an end. He was the first absolute monarch of this land after the Saxon conquest, which was a source of great joy to St. Cuthbert's monks. They now had the respect of a king who was willing and able to protect them, who dearly loved St Cuthbert and who made more princely donations to them than any previous king. The monks brought Aethelstan to such an excess of unseemly devotion, that he even made a barefoot pilgrimage to St. Cuthbert's shrine.

The monks must have had a good laugh when they met together (like magicians when they meet together), to see the monarchy so captivated by superstition, and majesty so humiliated, when the end result of their pretended sanctity was only their own laziness and fatness.

When this devout king was leading an army into Scotland, he made a diversion to St. Cuthbert's sepulchre. There he begged for the saint's aid, and asked him to be his patron in wartime. He used many princely gifts to buy the good wishes of the monks, and their blessings on his journey.

At the king's command, his soldiers also offered £96 in silver at St. Cuthbert's tomb, at a time when it would have been more fitting for St Cuthbert to give them that amount out of the church's treasury. The soldiers were, after all, just about to win a victory for their king, with their swords and their own blood. But St. Cuthbert and his lazy, idle monks had to claim the glory of the subsequent victory by saying that their blessings had caused it. The monks, of course, preferred to sleep with their skins intact, and not marked with battle-scars.

King Edmund (Aethelstan's brother) believed this claim, and he also

---

13 England was divided into 7 kingdoms until this time: Northumbria, Mercia, East Anglia, Kent, Essex, Wessex and Sussex.

visited St. Cuthbert on his way to Scotland, honouring his sepulchre with many kingly offerings. He also renewed the charters of his predecessors; with Vulcan's pot, and everlasting brimstone threatened for any who should break said charters.

Now, it may be convenient for the government of a country for some men to be thought by the common people to be powerful wizards, or warlocks, even though these men may be altogether guiltless of using magic. And people who trust God (and not other people) with their guilty secrets, might be more afraid to offend the church in case their secrets should be revealed. Likewise, a king might make good use of the reputation of St. Cuthbert as a tutelary deity against the Scots.

Because they believed in Cuthbert's help, the English soldiers were much encouraged (to the great disadvantage of their enemies) and won the war. As the Scots believed that Cuthbert was against them, they made fewer incursions into his lands. The monks also invented many frightening miracles, which were supposed to afflict those who used stealth or violence to attack anything that belonged to the saint.

I just wonder how the monks could keep up this deception for so many generations, when people were growing wiser all the time, and beginning to suspect that the monks were dishonest, and invented miracles for their own gain.

It seems that the monks had to work very hard to maintain the saintly reputations of both St. Cuthbert and St. Thomas à Becket. They pretended that there was such friendship between these two saints, that by way of exchange, sick people from St. Thomas's lands had to go and be healed by St.Cuthbert, and those from St. Cuthbert's lands had to be made better by St. Thomas à Becket. Of course, it was no problem for a a diseased person to travel from Canterbury to Durham, or from Durham to Canterbury.

The monks knew very well that some of these sick people would not be able to undertake the pilgrimage; that others would rather depend on the sainthood of a physician; that others would be content to die at home, others would recover spontaneously, and that some would die on their journey. It may be that, to protect the reputation of their saint, the monks would also make sure some sick people never got to his shrine at all.

For a long period, the monks and bishops at Chester-le-Street enjoyed such an easy and quiet time, they did not even get a mention in the chronicles. They began to feature in history again when rumours of more Danish landings disturbed their peace. By this time, the monks had been in Chester-le-Street for one hundred and fifteen years.

One night Aldwin, their Bishop (who had been schoolmaster to Edward the Confessor) was warned in his sleep by St. Cuthbert to avoid the fury of the Pagans by escaping with his coffin to Ripon. This the monks did, but after six months peace returned again.

As they returned from Ripon, a great miracle happened at Warde Law[14], east of Durham. There St. Cuthbert's coffin became so heavy, that all the people who attended the corpse could not pull the wagon on which it lay. From this they concluded that St Cuthbert did not want to return to Chester-le-Street.

At length, and after three days of fasting, it was revealed to Eadmar, a devout monk, that Durham was to be Cuthbert's final resting place. When they set off for Durham, they found that two or three people could draw the cart, which before, a whole diocese of people could not so much as move.

There is a common fable about a dun cow and a milk-maid that directed them to Durham, but I can find nothing about this in the histories, even though those authors would surely not have left out any miracles involving St Cuthbert.[15]

X: DURHAM

At that time Durham was naturally fortified by woods so thick that they prevented the stars from seeing the earth, and the earth from seeing heaven. Here the devoted monks improvised a shelter for Cuthbert, in the form of a sort of arbour of boughs and tree-branches. From this chapel of boughs, they later moved him into another church called the White Church. He rested there for three years, as in a chapel of rest.

In 990 Bishop Aldwin raised up a stone building of considerable size, as his cathedral church[16]. All the people between Coquet and Tees worked for three years on this project, and were paid with the expectation of treasure in heaven (a very cheap way to pay workmen).

St Cuthbert's body was at last enshrined in the new building, with great

---

14 Raine suggests Wardley (in Gateshead). Fowler thinks this cannot be Warden Law, east of Chester-le-Street.
15 Fowler claims this was first recorded in *The Rites of Durham* (1593).
16 This is usually called the Great Church, immediate predecessor of the present cathedral.

solemnity, three hundred and nine years after his first burial on Lindisfarne. This happened in the presence of Uthred, Earl of Northumberland.

Among the monks who followed St. Cuthbert to Durham was one called Regulf, who lived to the age of 210, which almost puts him in the same category as the Wandering Jew. Unfortunately Regulf doesn't seem to have achieved anything other than living for a very long time - nothing else is known about him. We might say that he existed for a very long time, but did he really live during all those years?

Another of St. Cuthbert's followers was Eadred, a monk who, for six years before he died, could only speak when he was in the church. There, as if religion had then given him a tongue, he sang more enthusiastically than anyone else.

These were the beginnings of the Church of Durham, where Aldwin (the last Bishop of Chester-le-Street and the first of Durham) first ascended his bishop's chair in 996. That was in the reign of King Ethelred, who, while St. Dunstan was baptising him, is said to have been sick in the font. At this, St. Dunstan swore by God and his mother, that he would prove a lazy fellow.

To maintain the laziness of the monks of Durham, Ethelred gave St. Cuthbert the town of Darlington, where later Hugh Pudsey built both a manor and a church. Snaculf, one of the nobility, added Bradbury, Mordon and Sockburn to these possessions. This shows how willing the religious people of the time were to give everything to the church, and make themselves poor. They did this in the hope of riches in the world to come. Perhaps the monks were the only people who were supposed to be happy both before and after death.

Aldwin died twenty-four years after he had moved to Durham, and left only the west tower of the church for Edmund, his successor, to finish.

Edmund had been chosen as bishop by a voice which spoke out of St Cuthbert's tomb (or perhaps by the voice of a monk who was a friend of Edmund's, and hid under the tomb). I think the latter is probably what happened, as I haven't read that Cuthbert, in the words of an old proverb, 'drank his porridge to speak in his grave'. But all joking aside, Edmund was a reverend prelate, who achieved more honour in his life than any of his predecessors.

The Danes, who had once burnt Cuthbert's church in Lindisfarne, now became worshippers of St. Cuthbert in Durham. They had converted from Pagans to Christians, and were in fact so devout that their king, Cnut, walked five miles barefoot to Cuthbert's tomb. It was as if he meant to make up for all the bad things his ancestors had done to the saint.

Cnut gave so many towns to St Cuthbert, it would make a fat monk breathless to repeat them. These included Wackerfield, Evenwood, Aycliffe, Lotherton, Ingleton, Middleton, Staindrop, and Raby. At Raby, the predecessors of the Nevilles (who are buried in the church at Staindrop) built a castle, and rented it from the church of Durham for the rent of £4 and a hart, to be paid annually.

The monks of Durham were now so well-off, and had such a fine church for their saint to rest in, they were ashamed he had ever lain at Chester-le-Street. The church there was still made of wood, and seemed to be a reminder of their former poverty. So Bishop Egelric took away this eyesore, and built a stone church in honour of St. Cuthbert. This was a compliment to St Cuthbert that came too late – like someone who is inhospitable to a guest when he is in his house, and only gets a nice room ready for him after he's gone.

While they were digging the foundations of this new church, they found such a massive hoard of coins that Egelric resigned his bishopric to his brother Egelwin, and returned to his abbey at Peterborough. The king, however, heard of his sudden wealth and deliberately picked a quarrel with him. He then seized all his riches and imprisoned him at Westminster; because of course it is a great crime for a man to be rich, when his sovereign wants money. This king (if you want to know his name) was William the Conqueror.

When William was approaching York with an army, he frightened the monks of Durham so much, they put St. Cuthbert on their backs once again. They hurried off to Lindisfarne, staying at Jarrow on the first night, at Bedlington on the second, at Tughall on the third, and at Holy Island itself on the fourth night.

They were able to cross to Lindisfarne on foot, since it happened to be low tide; but of course they said this was like the miracle of the River Jordan or the Red Sea, and that the waters had parted for them as an act of homage to the saint they carried.

The monks' fear of King William proved to be unfounded, and they soon returned again to Durham.

When the Conqueror was coming back from Scotland with his army, he insisted on seeing the miraculously preserved remains of the famous saint. The monks had never been so afraid that their deception might be discovered! They had no time to cheat the king by substituting a living monk for the dead saint, so they stalled and delayed as much as they could. This made the king so angry that he developed a fever and had to rush out of the church and ride off. The monks later claimed that William continued to ride until he had crossed the River Tees, where his fever left him.

To be revenged on the monks, the king soon tried to abrogate the charters they held from previous monarchs. He also sent a tax-collector to extract money from the tenants of Cuthbert's lands. Cuthbert came to this man in his sleep, and beat him so badly with his bishop's crook that he couldn't get up the next morning. The tax-collector didn't even start to get better until he had sent his own cloak as a gift to Cuthbert's tomb, and begged the monks to forgive him. The monks preserved this famous cloak for many years.

After this, the king started to have more respect for St. Cuthbert, and restored Billingham, and other villages, to the church. He also gave Bishop Walcher of Durham the title of Earl of Northumberland. In this way, the monks conquered the Conqueror, and used their religion to subdue the man who had subdued the whole land with his sword.

XI: THE CATHEDRAL

'Cuthbert's end' of Durham Cathedral

At this time the the church of Durham was growing to the height of its glory, under that magnificent prelate, William of Carilef. William thought the church Aldwin had put up was too little for so great a saint, so in the hundredth year after it was built, it was demolished, and the foundations of a larger church were laid. This is the cathedral we see today.

King Malcolm of Scotland, the Bishop himself, and Prior Turgot laid the first stones of the new cathedral on August 11th, 1093. Anthony Beak, one of Bishop William's successors, paid a great deal of money to have him canonized and enrolled among the saints, because he had built such a great cathedral.

This reverend old cathedral stands on the shoulders of a vast hill, and is surrounded by more hills. Anyone who has seen this city has seen a map of Zion, and may save himself a journey to the Holy Land. The city is almost completely enclosed by the renowned River Wear, in which, as in a mirror, the city might once have seen the beauty of her walls. Now, she only sees the ruins of her walls.

Into this sumptuous church was the last and greatest translation of St. Cuthbert.

Prior Turgot and his brethren had a great desire to confirm with their own eyes the tradition of the miraculous preservation of Cuthbert's body. If the body was still preserved, they planned to show it publically on the day of the move. So at night the Prior, with seven of his brethren, met at the tomb and reverently took off the covering-stone.

Inside, they found a chest covered with leather, which had been fastened on with nails. This was enclosed by another coffin with two covers, wrapped six times round with a cloth. In the cloth they found the book of the gospels, which had fallen into the sea. They also found a little silver altar, a goblet of pure gold with an onyx stone, and an ivory comb. Opening the third chest, they looked upon the flesh and body of their saint.

He was lying on his right side, to make space for the rest of the relics. These were so numerous that Cuthbert's coffin seemed like a charnel-house of bones.

Besides Cuthbert's own body, there were the bones of the Venerable Bede, the head of Saint Oswald and some of the bones of Aidan, Eadfrid, and Ethelwald, who had all been bishops of Lindisfarne.

The monks took out all of these relics with due reverence and placed them in other parts of the church. They then laid St. Cuthbert on his back, placing St. Oswald's head between his hands.

On the fourth of September, the day of Cuthbert's translation, Bishop Ranulf preached his resurrection sermon instead of conducting a funeral, and told the people about the miraculous preservation of St Cuthbert's body.

After four hundred and eighteen years the body was still flexible, and might with justice make an argument for its own immortality.

They enshrined Cuthbert behind the High Altar, with great ceremony, in the presence of the Abbots of St. Alban's, Sees[17], St. Mary's of York and St. German's, together with thousands of other people, who were all witnesses of the miracle.

This was Cuthbert's last place of rest. So many treasures were offered here every day that the monks didn't need to study alchemy to get gold, since they already had a philosopher's stone to put money into their purses. Their philosopher's stone was of course Cuthbert's tombstone.

Cuthbert's shrine had such a holy reputation, and so many worshippers, that to this day you can still see the pious scars of ancient devotion: the very stones near the tomb are guttered and worn out with kneeling.

St. Cuthbert slept here for four hundred years without disturbance, except that once he complained in a dream to a monk, of a mouse who had made her nest in his tomb. She alone troubled his rest.

---

17 In NW France.

34

Four hundred years after the translation of St Cuthbert, King Henry VIII caused an earthquake among the monasteries, and the tombs of the saints, by ordering that they be opened up in search of treasure, as Darius had opened the tomb of Semiramis[18].

Harpfield tells us that Cuthbert's tomb was also broken up, with so little respect that 'with the violence of the blow upon the coffin, they wounded his leg'.

They found that the whole body was complete except for the tip of the nose: not bad for a carcass that had lacked a soul for more than eight hundred years. Even Cuthbert's grave-clothes were so free from decay, it was as if they had been kept in a wardrobe rather than a sepulchre.

On his finger he had a ring with a sapphire in it: an unusual ornament for a dead man, but fitting for Cuthbert; it was as if this ring married him to his miraculous preservation. Henry's men didn't dare take the ring off, and left the tomb as it was, at the command of Bishop Tunstall.

The witnesses to all this included Doctor Whitehead (Prior of Durham), William Whitham (the keeper of Cuthbert's shrine), Doctor Spark, Doctor Todd, and others belonging to the cathedral.

It may be that Cuthbert was well-preserved, but for reasons other than his own saintliness. The skill of the monks who embalmed him might be the reason. In ancient times, the Egyptians embalmed the bodies of their dead kings, using wrappings to preserve their carcases for many centuries. These kings were not regarded as saints, as Cuthbert was, and Paracelsus was not thought to be a god, just because he made a vegetable man without a soul.[19]

Until the time of Edward I, no one dared to be buried in the same church as St Cuthbert: nobody was thought worthy enough to lie under the same roof as such a miraculously preserved saint. Because of this, the most ancient monuments and historical tombstones in the Cathedral precincts are to be found in the chapter house. Here you will find the tomb of Bishop Walcher, Earl of Northumberland and first Count Palatine of Durham.

---

18 In Plutarch's *Moralia*.
19 The alchemist Paracelsus (1493-1541) claimed to have created a homunculus, or miniature man, during a bizarre experiment.

Cuthbert's skull, as seen by James Raine in 1827 (JR)

Walcher built the ancient infirmary for the monks of Jarrow. He also moved these monks from Jarrow to Durham, having first obtained a special licence from Pope Gregory VII. Walcher was murdered in the church at Gateshead, and Odo, Bishop of Bayeux, was sent over to avenge his death. Odo's medicine proved too strong, however: he not only killed a lot of people; he also stole from the church, and even commandeered the Bishop's beautifully-made crozier staff.

William of Carilef, who built the Cathedral, also lies buried in the chapter house, and between him and Walcher lies the learned Prior Turgot, Archdeacon of Durham (afterwards Bishop of St. Andrew's in Scotland). He also wrote about the history of Durham Cathedral.

I have missed out some of the chapter house monuments because I need to go back and check them. I do remember that there is a monument to the magnificent Hugh Pudsey, King Stephen's nephew. He founded the Priory of Finchale in honour of St Godric, who had lived there as a hermit.

XII: GODRIC

Because Godric is one of the local saints, I will tell you about him. My source is a book written by Nicholas, a monk at the Priory of Finchale.

In his younger days St Godric had been a pedlar, and carried his portable shop on his back from fair to fair. Later, he travelled to Flanders, Denmark and Scotland to make his fortune.

He used to visit Holy Island, and there he loved to hear the monks tell stories about St Cuthbert. These tales affected him so deeply that he felt he had to make a pilgrimage to the Holy Land. On his return, Cuthbert came to him in a dream and persuaded him to go again. This time, he visited the Holy Sepulchre and washed his feet in the Jordan. He left his shoes by the Jordan, and vowed to go barefoot for the rest of his life.

When he returned to Britain for the second time, St Cuthbert came to Godric in his sleep and told him to build an anchorage at Finchale. There he built a cell of thatch, which he dedicated to the Virgin Mary.

He lived so religiously, he even used to pray while standing up to his neck in the river that ran by his cell. This enraged the Devil so much that he stole Godric's clothes from the bank. But Godric saw this, and forced the devil to come back and replace the clothes by saying, 'Praise Mary'. These clothes were, however, so uncomfortable that the Devil would probably have been quite unable to wear them.

Godric's jerkin was made of iron - in fact he wore out three such jerkins while he was living as a hermit. This was a strange sort of jerkin for him to wear, not least because his draper must have been an iron-monger, and his tailor a blacksmith.

His house was just as uncomfortable as his jerkin: he had the ground for his bed, and a stone for his pillow. His tutelary angel often acted as his sexton, and rang a bell to wake him for his nocturns[20].

The saint didn't have a rosary, so he used pebbles to count his prayers. His shirt was made of sackcloth, and his diet was as coarse as his clothes: his bread was made up of a mixture of flour and ashes.

The Devil used to act like Proteus[21] before Godric, but his different shapes didn't frighten the saint at all – they just amused him.

Once, as St. Godric sat by the fire, the Devil came up behind and gave

---

20 Monastic offices (prayers and/or services) performed at night.
21 Ancient Greek sea-god who could change his shape at will.

him such a box on the ears that he might have died; but he healed himself by making the sign of the cross.

Godric always had the book of Psalms hanging from his little finger, so that eventually this finger became permanently crooked. After acting out this legend of miracles, Godric ended his scene and his life in the year 1170: he didn't really deserve to have his cell made into a full-scale abbey by Bishop Hugh Pudsey.

The River Wear near Godric's cell at Finchale

Godric had told Bishop Hugh that he would be blind for seven years before he died. The bishop believed the saint and delayed his repentance until he should start to go blind, which never happened. It turned out that Godric had meant that the *eyes of Hugh's understanding* would be blind, so the bishop was quite unprepared for death, when it came.

To judge from Hugh Pudsey's good deeds, however, he didn't really need to repent. He repaired many of the episcopal manors, built Darlington Church, and founded the hospitals at Allerton, and at Sherburn near Durham. He also built Elvet Bridge over the Wear at Durham, together with its two chapels.

Hugh Pudsey also bought from King Richard I the earldom of Sadberge for his successors, and built the beautiful Galilee or Lady Chapel of Durham Cathedral (now called the Consistory[22]). He caused the bones of the Venerable Bede to be moved into this chapel, where they now lie under a tomb of black marble, without an inscription[23].

Elvet Bridge

XIII: MONUMENTS

I assume that the great bell[24] in the cathedral is named after the Galilee chapel. This may be the same bell that, according to an old manuscript, was drawn from London to Durham by twenty-two oxen.

Under the Consistory table is the tomb of Cardinal Langley, Bishop of Durham and Lord Chancellor of England, who built both the music and the grammar schools.

In the choir in front of the high altar lies Bishop Beaumont, under a large piece of marble inlaid with brass. Some say he built the city walls of

22 Then used as a Consistory Court; a bishop's court dealing with ecclesiastical law.
23 There is an inscription now, which reads 'HIC SUNT IN FOSSA BAEDAE VENERABILIS OSSA' (here lie the Venerable Bede's bones in a trench). This was added after the investigation of Bede's tomb in 1831.
24 From the 13th century, the belfry had 4 bells, called Galilee, Long Bell, St Oswald and St Bede.

Durham. Beside him lies the famous Bishop Anthony Beak, Patriarch of Jerusalem, who was also Prince of the Isle of Man. According to Leland he built the manor of Auckland, repaired Barnard and Alnwick Castles, and made Chester-le-Street a collegiate church, with a dean and seven prebends.

Very few ancient monuments of women are to be found in the cathedral, because until recent times no female was supposed to enter any church belonging to St. Cuthbert. This is because once, as he was a preaching, the Devil came to hear his sermon in the shape of a very beautiful woman. This vision distracted Cuthbert's listeners, until he threw holy water on the woman and revealed what she was.

But Cuthbert himself didn't dislike the company of his holy sisters. Hilda, Aelfflaed, Verca, Aebba, and other abbesses, were his intimate acquaintance; and if he had disliked the female sex, he would not have built a nunnery at Carlisle.

In his young days, Cuthbert was even accused of seducing the daughter of the King of the Picts – but of course this was the Devil disguised as Cuthbert.

But to return. In the choir on the north side Bishop Skirlaw lies under a handsome brass monument. He built the cathedral cloisters, as well as two great bridges over the Wear at Newton and Shincliff. He also built a third bridge over the Tees at Yarm, the steeple of Holm Church[25], and a great part of the lantern of York Minster. He donated two hundred pounds for the building of the diribitory at Durham, which I think must be the exchequer[26] over the cathedral gates.

There were as many relics in this cathedral as there are saints in the Pope's list. At the resurrection, St Giles will collect his tooth from there, St Zacharias will fetch his leg, another saint his hip-bone, another his skull, another his knuckle-bone, besides a whole wardrobe of saint's clothes, including coats and hoods, and stockings of the apostles. There are also many pieces of the true cross and of the sacred sepulchre.

If you would like to know the price relics were sold for in those days, you can ask William of Malmesbury what Egolnoth, Archbishop of Canterbury, paid for St Augustine's arm. He bought this at Pavia, on his

---

25 Possibly Holme St Cuthbert in Cumbria.
26 The Chamberlain's Exchequer, to the NW of the Gatehouse. Later rebuilt. In his notes for *The Rites of Durham*, Fowler says 'diribitory' is a mistake for 'dormitory'.

way back from Rome, and William will tell you that it cost him a hundred talents of silver and one talent of gold. Egolnoth was shown up as a fool by this bargain, and we know from Pliny that 'a bad bargain vexes a man, chiefly because it seems a strong instance of his folly'[27].

The funniest of all the relics at Durham is this one: a monk called Elfrid had got hold of one of St Cuthbert's hairs, which, when laid on hot coals would become red hot, but would return to its former colour when it was taken off. So, not so much as a hair of St Cuthbert could escape the monks without a miracle.

Among other monuments in the cathedral, the brass lectern is not the least. This was the joint gift of a reverend prebend of the church and his son. They added the globe and the eagle to a sumptuous column and its base. The column was originally part of a large candlestick, found hidden in a vault of the church. The prebend and his son both lie buried under marble stones inlaid with brass, on your left hand as you enter the choir. This part of the church is almost completely paved with the grave-stones of my own close relatives.

The subterranean passages under this cathedral are, as in other abbeys, numerous. Whether these were built as places to conceal treasure during invasions, or for worse purposes, I cannot determine. It is certain that the cathedral and the castle shake hands underground by means of these passages.

XIV: THE CASTLE

The castle was built by William the Conqueror for the defence of the city. The iron gate was set up by Bishop Tunstall, who also built the city's toll-booth, and had water piped into his palace and the cathedral. The castle's tower was repaired by Richard Fox, afterwards Bishop of Winton. He also founded Corpus Christi College, Oxford, of which I am a member.

In the chapel of Corpus Christi College there were once two altars, one called *ara Trinitis*, the other *ara Sancti Cuthberti*, which suggests that St Cuthbert was Bishop Fox's saint.

Philip of Poitou, Bishop of Durham, had a licence from Richard I to set up a mint, and make money in the castle.

The whole of Durham Castle has now been repaired and beautifully

---

27 Pliny, Epistle XXIV, trans. by John Boyle Orrery.

adorned (and lit up by many windows) by the present reverend bishop.

Under this bishop[28], the Church of Durham seems to grow young again, and to take a new lease of eternity. The cathedral can now challenge her sister churches with the beauty of her high altar, her cathedral music, her sacred laver[29] and other ornaments.

Thus, like a man trying to say hello to many people at once, I have made a confused survey of the monuments of this church, with such brevity and lack of method, that I feel I have taken an inventory of her antiquities, rather than compiled a history. I offer it 'as is' upon one of the altars the Romans used to erect with this inscription,

Diis Patriis,

To the spirit of my country

---

28 Richard Neile (1562-1640)
29 Perhaps the ' fair laver or counditt for ye mounckes to wash ther hands & faces at' (*Rites of Durham*).

FURTHER READING

Bede: *A history of the English church and people*, Penguin, 1986

Bertram Colgrave: *Two lives of St Cuthbert*, Cambridge, 1985

Frank Stenton: *Anglo-Saxon England*, Oxford, 1971

J.F. Webb and D.H. Farmer: *The age of Bede*, Penguin, 2004

Also by Simon Webb:

In Search of the Little Count:

Joseph Boruwlaski, Durham Celebrity

ISBN 978-0-9544759-5-6